FLORAL ART FOR AMERICA

In the Flemish Manner (see page 33)

Floral Art for America

By Martha Ryan Lowry

PHOTOGRAPHY BY HAROLD CORSINI

M. Barrows and Company, Inc. New York

To my mother and father

and

To my children and grandchildren

Preface

During the last thirty years flower arrangement has had a new and eventful history in America. In this brief time it has achieved unprecedented popularity and has indeed been rediscovered as an art. The disciplines of technique, design, and style in floral art are widely understood and taught now as never before. And, as with all creative endeavor, different and often opposing schools of thought about it have evolved.

Martha Ryan Lowry has participated in the development of this new art since the beginning, arranging for her own home and for exhibitions, teaching, lecturing, and arranging professionally as well. She has explored the endless possibilities of plant material and studied the influence on floral art of style and design in other arts of the past and present and of many cultures. And she has not hesitated to make new departures; in this her work is truly creative and reflects the freedom and variety that are typical of floral art in America. It is rare, in fact, that any one arranger can encompass so many different ways of designing with plant material and can offer so much that is fresh and entirely her own.

Mrs. Lowry concentrates in this collection on arrangements for one's own home. Her themes alternately express charm, humor, elegance, and great simplicity. But she also displays a sure sense of what is appropriate in arranging for exhibition or in modern office buildings or adapting intricate period designs. To achieve such a broad range she has worked in a variety of styles that to some may even appear to belong to conflicting traditions. But the guiding principle in every arrangement is respect for the nature of plant material and awareness of its intrinsic beauty. This is the essence of floral art that concerns all arrangers.

THE PUBLISHERS

Contents

LIST OF ILLUSTRATIONS

Color Plates

Black-and-white Plates

Acknowledgments

I am immeasurably grateful to my wonderful family and friends for their patience, co-operation, encouragement and interest, expressed generously so many times in so many ways. To the late Mrs. Roy A. Hunt, for her encouragement and advice; to Mr. Walter Read Hovey, head of the Henry Clay Frick Fine Arts Department of the University of Pittsburgh for his approval and assistance; to my wonderful friend, Mr. Thomas D. Jolly who made possible so many of my assignments, and to Mr. Frederick J. Close whose enthusiasm and guidance made these assignments become a reality, my deep gratitude; to Mr. Ray Tucker whose unfailing interest over the years shall never be forgotten; to Mary Lee Kennedy White, for her understanding and faith and for her beautiful "Madonna and Child" sculptured in wood; to Art and Elsie Rippl, who have kept my interest in flower arranging always in mind and have brought me such interesting material; to Betty Abel, who generously shared her own artistic talent and who has stood by with help when needed; to Sue and Jim Kinnear, who made possible the lovely fresh plant material from their southern garden which I have used in so many arrangements; to Eleanor Knabe, for unfailing interest and encouragement; to Sara Mundo for her advice and guidance; to Larry Vollmer, of Joseph Horne Company, who for many years has aided and abetted my efforts; to Mr. Joseph H. Proudfoot, III, of S. S. Pennock Company for his marvelous co-operation in supplying only the freshest and loveliest of plant materials; to Charles Wise, Mt. Lebanon florist, for his co-operation; to the Trax family, whose fine farm furnished me with the finest of vegetables and gourds and who always granted me the privilege of selecting and choosing; to the Hickman Gardens, where I snipped and cut as though they were mine; to Tony Battaglia, my loyal fruit man, for perfect fruit in season or out of season.

For four of the photographs in this book I am indebted to the studios of Boutrelle-Sevecke, New York (Plate 11), and Associated Photographers, Pittsburgh (Plates 34, 63, and 93).

My gratitude to Mr. Elmer A. Lundberg for making possible our use of the beautiful cullet shown on Plate 91. Grateful, too, am I to Margaret Fairbanks Marcus, whose book *Period Flower Arrangement* was a constant reference for Part I and whose research saved me untold time and energy.

My personal thanks to the great garden club organizations in America—the Garden Club of America, the National Council of State Garden Clubs, Inc., the state garden club associations, and garden centers; men and women, experts in the field of horticulture, floriculture, and conservation, each of them dedicated to making America more beautiful, to conserving its beauty, and to bringing into the daily lives of all of us the great therapeutic and spiritual value found in Nature upon which our entire existence depends.

To my sister, Ethel M. Ryan, without whose faith, knowledge, and affection this book could never have been accomplished, I owe a special debt of gratitude.

And finally, the great opportunity of having my finished work photographed by one of our nationally known photographers, Harold Corsini, has been a rewarding experience. Also, to his wonderful staff, George Cooper, Jim Papariello, and Rae Shortly for their untiring effort, skill, and knowledge and their enthusiasm and respect for beauty, my grateful thanks.

MARTHA RYAN LOWRY

INTRODUCTION

The Art of Flower Arrangement and the Art of Awareness

The art of flower arrangement is a visual art. But what is the art of awareness?
The art of awareness is seeing,—seeing with an inner eye that stimulates, through vision, some deeper feeling which we attribute to the heart.

Awareness is seeing the color of the sea as it rolls in to shore.
The color of the sea as it rolls in to shore.
It is seeing abstract sculpture in a sea shell.
It is seeing sculpture in a branch against a wintery sky.
It is seeing beauty in wood that has been twisted and turned by the tide.
It is seeing expression in the faces of flowers.
It is seeing texture in a leaf.
It is seeing rhythm in the stems of flowers as they hold up their heads.
It is seeing massiveness in a great boulder.
It is seeing form in fruit and vegetables.
It is seeing the architectural structure of a pine cone.
It is seeing and feeling a poem in a pine tree against a sky of blue.

It is seeing the basic relationship of all things to Nature and striving to discover Nature's unexplained mysteries.

All this and ever so much more lies within every one of us, ready to awaken when the desire to create demands fulfillment.

I believe in this beauty that I see, hear, and feel around me. We all have access to it in plant material, in flowers—colorful, fragile, sculptured, changing, and exquisite. This is *my* chosen medium.

Perhaps we are afraid of our emotions, perhaps the tempo of our lives is too swift, our minds too impatient, perhaps we are too timid to admit the need of self-expression. But when we do find a medium that fits our needs—and use it—then into our lives come fulfillment and a sense of peace. I believe that beauty is a necessity, that if we see beauty, feel beauty, think and express it, that this world may become a better place in which to live.

For a long time homemakers have felt the need of a book of floral art—a book designed for the American home in the American way; a pictorial book that would enable them, without too much study and research, to create flower arrangements for their own homes. This is the kind of book I have tried to create; one that fills a personal need.

To all homemakers I humbly present my book, compiled with a minimum of text and without restrictions or rules. It is my hope that the designs will speak for themselves. If I can share this wonderful art and beauty with but a few I shall be content, grateful for the health and guidance that have permitted me to finish this task.

For the pure joy of living let us bring our flowers into our homes, in sickness and sadness, joy and gladness, and let them speak for us when words come not too readily to our lips.

Part One

IN RETROSPECT

IN RETROSPECT

The study of ancient cultures tells us that people ever since civilization began have been appreciative of Nature and her gifts. We know, too, that many of our flowers of today date back as far as 2500 B.C.; that flowers were used not alone for decorative purposes but were associated with the seasons and used as offerings to the gods. Long before man could express abstract ideas in words or pictures, he chose flowers to speak for him, making a symbolic language of them.

The art of flower arrangement as we know it today was first introduced to America in the 1930s, although some garden clubs prior to that time had shown interest in composing flowers in vases. In 1931, the Federated Garden Clubs of New York State, Inc., held its first annual Judging Course, an event that caused nationwide interest among floriculturists and horticulturists alike. In 1943, the great organization, The National Council of State Garden Clubs, Inc., sponsored Judging Schools that today are known as Flower Show Schools and these schools have spread like wildfire across our country.

Thus began a new art in America and it seemed natural that this new art should turn to an older one for guidance. Records of floral art in Europe prior to the seventeenth century were few and difficult to obtain, but hundreds of beautiful flower paintings of the Dutch, Flemish, and French artists dating from that time could easily be found in museums and private collections throughout the world. Thus, the seventeenth century became a starting place in this country for the study of the European flower art.

It was a fascinating research to study the paintings of these fine Dutch, Flemish and French artists. While we recognized that the paintings are sometimes not of actual flowers but are only the artists' concepts of flowers, we also recognized that these great masters had a profound knowledge of botany as well as horticulture. What a source of inspiration and beauty! How well they knew how to assemble and organize many varieties as well as great quantities of material into opulent masses of exquisite color.

We also turned to the other side of the world for guidance and discovered from the traditions of China and Japan a wealth of knowledge and inspiration. From China we learned the importance of the living line, seasonal appropriateness, symbolism, and of the elegance of plant material, containers, and appurtenances. From Japan, a country where the arranging of flowers has been a recognized art for centuries up to the present, we found a vast amount of literature, and schools, styles, and techniques for study. Perhaps Japan's greatest contribution to arranging has been emphasis on design and on sensitivity to the beauties of growing plants.

As we strive today to apply our knowledge of period designs and to show this great influence of the past, we make very little attempt to achieve authenticity other than to select material that was available in that century or to substitute modern materials which are in the spirit of the time. Also, we strive to obtain either an authentic container or a reproduction of one.

Now, after a quarter of a century of study, trial, and error, we see emerging an American way with flowers. Conscious of design and the past, and yet wishing to express the beauty and abundance of our great land, the art of flower arrangement in America has just begun. We owe our best efforts to this great dual heritage.

MATERIALS:
  Boxwood
  Broom corn
  Chrysanthemums
  Papyrus
  Spathodea pods

CONTAINER: Reproduction of an Egyptian vase—
  copper overlaid with silver
MECHANICS: Crumpled wire mesh partly fills vase
BASE: Cork
SIZE: *Height*: 32 inches, *Width*: 26 inches

PLATE 1

In the Egyptian Manner

Inspired by the floral art of ancient Egypt—a land of gentle, gracious people. In their design of flowers the Egyptians valued order. Even rows of flowers collared their vases. Each row of flowers was one color—never mixed.

Light tan papyrus nestling in dark brown broom corn that has been severely pruned makes a harmonious backdrop for the small yellow mums. Dark blue velvet ribbon separates the rows of flowers. Shiny green boxwood and the black spathodea pods add interest.

PLATE 2

In the Grecian Manner

In this design an accessory becomes an integral part of the composition. A beautiful Grecian figurine gazes thoughtfully into an urn of roses and violets. The garland is the Norse fire plant which grows in long streamers of tiny shiny green leaves. Placed on a glass-topped table, the reflection adds great beauty.

MATERIALS:
    Ferns   Roses—Garnet
    Figurine   Violets
    Norse fire plant

CONTAINER: Alabaster urn
MECHANICS: Needlepoint holder
BASE: Marble squares
SIZE: *Height:* 18 inches, *Width:* 12 inches

PLATE 3

The Roman Era

Inspired by a sculptured garland found on a marble sacrificial altar in the temple of Vespasianus, Pompeii—a garland of nuts, fruit, and leaves sculptured in A.D. 62. This garland and garlands of later periods have been full of inspiration for our present-day needs, especially for Christmas decorations. Wired on a chain of straw links, this one is pliable and easily hung. The ends are lovely old bronze scones discovered in an antique shop.

MATERIALS:

Acorns	Jacaranda pods
Apples	Magnolia pods
Chestnuts	Peach stones
Cones—pine and spruce	Piñon cones
Eucalyptus pods	Sweet gum balls
Hickory nuts	Strelitzia leaves, dried

SIZE: *Length:* 44 inches

25

MATERIALS:
   Carnations
   Heather

CONTAINER: Black and gold compote
MECHANICS: Oasis and wire mesh
SIZE: *Height:* 32 inches, *Width:* 12 inches

PLATE 4

From the Byzantine Mosaics

A solid cone of carnations in the Byzantine style would make a charming design for a formal occasion. A cone of wire mesh filled with water-soaked Oasis was used for the foundation and secured to the bowl of the container. Carnation stems were cut in uniform length and stuck into the Oasis. Starting at the bottom, a perfect cone can easily be attained. The material at the top is heather. Any round-form flower can be substituted: marigolds, asters, zinnias, or chrysanthemums.

MATERIALS:
    Camphor pods
    Chamaecyparis—false cypress
    Chestnuts
    Coconut calyx
    Cones—spruce and larch
    Crab apples
    Deodar pods
    Eucalyptus pods
    Hickory nuts
    Sweet gum pods
    Walnuts

MECHANICS: Two 20-inch wire wreaths wired together furnish a strong base on which to wire the material.

SIZE: *Height:* 26 inches, *Width:* 26 inches

PLATE 5

Renaissance

Terra-cotta figure of Mother and Child within a wreath of cones, nuts, fruits, and flowers inspired by the designs of the Della Robbia family of the Renaissance period, late fifteenth and early sixteenth centuries.

Today in many parts of our country "nut wreaths" have become a traditional part of our Christmas. They last for many years and if sprayed with liquid furniture polish a lovely patina develops which enhances the color of the material. It also helps to preserve the nuts and cones.

All material must be wired and the nuts must be drilled and wired. Note how the grouping of the same materials creates a more pleasing design. Scale of material is important. Small artificial fruit and flowers have been added for color. The evergreen at the base is false cypress, or chamaecyparis.

PLATE 6

In the Oriental Manner

An interpretation of the *Rikkwa* style, the word meaning "standing-up plant material." *Rikkwa* was the first formal style of Japanese floral art and was introduced by a Buddhist priest of the *Ikenobo* school. It was used in altar designs for Buddhist temples—rigid, dignified, and voluminous, to be in harmony with the lofty temple building. The container here is the lower half of an *usubata,* a Japanese bronze container used for classical arrangements.

To me this is a fascinating Oriental style and one that I should like very much to study. The long leaf branch of the Maki podocarpus seems to have fallen forward.

MATERIALS:

Aralia leaves	Pine branch	CONTAINER: Lower part of a bronze *usubata*
Boxwood	Podocarpus	BASE: None—shown on a wooden pedestal
Broom	Wisteria branch	SIZE: *Height*: 46 inches, *Width*: 48 inches
Chrysanthemums	Yucca	

PLATE 7

In the French Rococo Manner

Fruit can be arranged in a delightful composition that shows the influence of the European rococo style of the eighteenth century.

An old lamp base was topped with a silver bread tray. A small green stick was placed diagonally across the tray and held in place with floral clay, then heavy bunches of grapes were wired to each end of the stick. This is the first operation. Next, seasonal fruit was snugly fitted to fill the tray. The pineapplelike foliage is billbergia. The foliage keeps fresh for several days without water if it has been first conditioned by soaking in water overnight.

MATERIALS:

Bananas	Pears	CONTAINER: Lamp base and silver bread tray
Billbergia	Plums	MECHANICS: Green stick and clay
Grapes		SIZE: *Height:* 21 inches, *Width:* 13½ inches
Limes		

MATERIALS:
  Allium
  Apples
  Apple blossoms
  Carnations
  Delphinium
  Doronicum
  Fritillaria—Crown Imperial
  Grapes
  Iris
  Mertensia
  Narcissi
  Pansies
  Parrot tulips
  Peony foliage
  Pineapple
  Primroses
  Ranunculus
  Roses
  Snapdragons
  Statice
  Tradescantia

CONTAINER: Lamp base—marble and bronze
MECHANICS: Large needlepoint holder
SIZE: *Height:* 40 inches, *Width:* 30 inches

PLATE 8

In the Flemish Manner

This design is shown in color on the Frontispiece. Inspired by the paintings of the old masters whose concepts of plant material arranged in great masses of exquisite color remain beautiful and challenging.

PLATE 9

In the French Manner

A mass arrangement of spring flowers designed for a special occasion.

MATERIALS:

Columbine	Phlox	CONTAINER: Alabaster urn
Coral bells	Primroses	ACCESSORIES: French satin ribbon
Doronicum	Roses	Antique French fan
Lilacs—French	Scillas	MECHANICS: Needlepoint holder
Lilacs—Persian	Snapdragons	SIZE: *Height*: 29 inches, *Width*: 21 inches
Lilies of the valley	Statice	
Pansies	Tulips	

PLATE 10

In the Manner of the English Georgian Period

A formal arrangement that expresses elegance and abundance in a mass composition somewhat triangular in form. A design used today in an elegant setting or for a special event.

MATERIALS:

Anemones
Carnations
Heather
Iris
Lilies

Lycoris
Roses
Snapdragons
Tulips

CONTAINER: Antique French urn
MECHANICS: Needlepoint and wire mesh
SIZE: *Height:* 33 inches, *Width:* 26 inches

MATERIALS:
  Grapes—Ribier
  Roses—miniature, yellow
  Roses—Orange Delight
  Peaches
  Violets

CONTAINER: Reed mat
BASE: Alabaster pedestal
MECHANICS: Cupped needlepoint holder
SIZE: *Height:* 30 inches, *Width:* 24 inches

PLATE 11

In the Manner of the Greek Classical Revival of 1762–1830

A tall, twin-columned stand of alabaster was selected to support a basket fashioned to represent a Grecian liknon. In Ancient Greece a liknon was the container chosen to hold fruit and flowers which, placed on a pedestal, were used as an offering to the gods.

A round rush mat, lavender in color, was pinned up on one side to approximate the shape of a liknon or fan-shaped basket. The roses follow the sloping line of the container, while violets and grapes spill over the edge. A charming design for a very special occasion.

MATERIALS:
  Fern
  Norse fire plant
  Peacock feathers
  Roses—Peace
  Roses—Floribunda—Fashion

CONTAINER: Twin-columned marble pedestal and marble urn
MECHANICS: Needlepoint holder
SIZE: *Height:* 40 inches, *Width:* 14 inches

PLATE 12

French Romantic Era

Inspired by the beauty of a nineteenth-century French panel of embroidered silk that is notable for its fabulous flower container of roses and its magnificent peacock.

MATERIALS:
  Crab apples
  Roses—Crimson Glory
  Roses—Garnet
  Viburnum tomentosum

CONTAINER: Alabaster epergne
MECHANICS: Needlepoint holder in top receptacle
  Aquapics
SIZE: *Height:* 24 inches, *Width:* 11 inches

PLATE 13

Victorian Romantic Era

A traditional design planned for a modern setting. An arrangement in an alabaster epergne—one of the most beautiful of containers—has been thoughtfully designed with particular awareness of two of the principles of design: proportion and balance, which are so apparent in the container itself. Careful attention was given to the selection of the material.

The roses, the crab apples, and the clusters of berries all had size relationship as well as beautiful color harmony. When completed, the composition had beauty, balance, contrast, rhythm, proportion, scale, simplicity, and color harmony.

MATERIALS:
Asters
Black-eyed Susans
Boltonia
Cattails
Dock
False dragonhead
Goldenrod
Hollyhocks
Marigolds
Milkweed pods
Petunias
Queen Anne's lace
Thistles
Zinnias

CONTAINER: Wooden butter bucket
MECHANICS: Oasis that has been soaked in water
SIZE: *Height:* 46 inches, *Width:* 27 inches

PLATE 14

Grandmother's Garden

Early Colonial period. An exhibit using flowers from Grandmother's garden just before the first frost.

PLATE 15

An Early Nineteenth-century Arrangement Designed for a Guest Room

MATERIALS:

Astilbe—pale pink
Coral bells
Maidenhair fern
Meadow rue (Thalictrum)—pale yellow
Pansies—rose, lavender, purple
Roses—Pink Bountiful

CONTAINER: Old glass lamp base
ACCESSORY: Chartreuse satin ribbon
MECHANICS: None. The arrangement was made in the hand and the stems inserted into the narrow opening of the lamp.
SIZE: *Height:* 25 inches, *Width:* 15 inches

44

Part Two

TODAY

TODAY

Who among us would attempt to select *one* design and claim that it alone represents the floral art of today in America? It would be an impossible task.

Today we live in an era of experimentation. Science has made available so much of everything that many of us find ourselves not only confused but also a bit frightened. We know that art in its many forms reflects the spirit of the time—its emotions, its progress, its poverty or abundance, to mention but a few of the essential qualities of any age. So it is in this medium of floral art.

Today we have Flower Show Schools that teach garden skills, knowledge of the science of horticulture, and show practices that enable garden clubs to present to their communities flower shows of high standards. In some of our larger cities garden clubs hold symposiums and present to their members speakers who are experts in their fields. We have great and small flower shows that are educational, stimulating, interesting, and very beautiful. In short, the art of flower arrangement has become an established art form, for the individual and the community.

And today we are able to obtain fresh plant material from any part of the world and have it delivered at our doorstep in breathtaking time. We have new color in flowers, new specimens, new varieties; fresh vegetables the year round and fruit that knows no season. We have exotic plants from other climes as well as unusual dried material available in our markets; new metals, new containers, fabulous glass, ceramics beyond description; wood from the mountain, from the seashore—sand-blasted, waxed, polished. As a result we are becoming a country with awareness of beauty never seen before. Color, color everywhere. How can one not be emotionally stirred!

But how can one be selective in the midst of this great abundance? And how can one avoid confusion? May I suggest one word, restraint! Don't try to cut every flower in your garden.

Don't buy quantities of material for fear you will not have enough. Plan your design. Know the space you plan to fill in your home with flowers: the dining-room table, the occasional table, the mantel, or the coffee table. Study the surroundings, the established color harmony, and then plan a design that is suitable and in good taste. With each success, a new world will be opened to you. You will no longer be just "fixing flowers"; you will be creating an arrangement of true art.

In good design lies the essence of beauty. All design is governed by the same principles: balance, dominance, contrast, rhythm, proportion, and scale.

To put these principles into practice, we use only two elements in our floral art: container and plant materials. With these elements we attain line, form, pattern, texture, and color—each of which must obey and implement the laws of design.

A flower arrangement that is organized according to these principles should attain beauty, simplicity, expression, and harmony.

Sounds simple, doesn't it? Well, it is—and wonderful!

A revealing test of whether a flower arranger has grasped the essential quality of floral art is in the use of the third, optional element, the accessory. It must add to the design, yet so often risks being merely an "extra something."

Unfortunately, all too often in our flower shows, we see an exhibit that has been erroneously classified as a flower arrangement. If the exhibit is contrived, distorted, an esoteric idea that ignores the essence of *floral* art, then, no matter how clever, how original it may be, it does not belong in a flower-arrangement class, for it pertains to a craft of another order and should be so classified. This we owe to the viewing public.

So let us accept today's challenge by increasing our awareness of beauty and trying to develop a style that will always be recognized as a design of American floral art.

MATERIALS:
  Iris
  Roses—Talisman
  Thalictrum
  Thalictrum foliage

CONTAINER: Anodized aluminum compote
BASE: Stainless steel
MECHANICS: Needlepoint holder
SIZE: *Height:* 30 inches, *Width:* 20 inches

PLATE 16

The Drama of Color

Contrary to the usual rule, the dark-colored flowers were used at the top of the arrangement with the lighter-colored flowers coming down into the bowl of the container. The perpendicular line is of dark purple iris; the diagonal line, light lavender thalictrum. The roses are Talisman and the lacy leaves are thalictrum foliage. Shown on a strip of stainless steel, the reflection adds interest.

PLATE 17 *(right)*

A Monochromatic Design

The seed pods of the lycoris, the loops of the yucca leaves, and the echeveria rosette were almost identical in their color value. Material beautifully sculptured by Nature.

MATERIALS:
    Echeveria
    Lycoris seed pods
    Yucca leaves

CONTAINER: Free-form black ceramic bowl
BASE: Black wood
MECHANICS: Needlepoint holder
SIZE: *Height:* 24 inches, *Width:* 9 inches

PLATE 18 *(opposite page)*

Large design using dried and fresh plant material. The cecropia leaves are of the species *Cecropia palmata*. These large leaves have from 7 to 11 lobes which curl when dried and show white beneath. They are magnificent! Cattails form a diagonal line on the left balanced by two of the cecropia leaves on the right. Large white mums give a dramatic fresh accent. The container is of Italian pottery in brown and white.

MATERIALS:
    Cattails
    Cecropia leaves
    Chrysanthemums—white

CONTAINER: Italian pottery vase
MECHANICS: Wire mesh and Aquapics
SIZE: *Height:* 34 inches, *Width:* 29 inches

MATERIALS:
  Gypsophila—white
  Monarch daisies—white

CONTAINER: Chinese vase
BASE: Teakwood
MECHANICS: Oasis that has been soaked in water
SIZE: *Height*: 35 inches, *Width*: 33 inches

PLATE 19

Five Monarch daisies display their beauty and size as they come marching down through a haze of white gypsophila. Almost like a sunbeam through a white cloud.

MATERIALS:
  Iris—Japanese—white
  Iris foliage

CONTAINER: Two-toned ceramic bowl, Oriental in
  design
BASE: Teakwood
MECHANICS: Needlepoint holder
SIZE: *Height:* 30 inches, *Width:* 16 inches

PLATE 20

Two flowers and two buds of the Japanese iris are all that is needed to make this delightfully simple design. The thin bladelike foliage of the iris contrasts well with the lovely flowers almost in full bloom.

PLATE 21

Simplicity and Restraint

Two spikes of delphinium and one branch of manzanita.

MATERIALS:
 Delphinium
 Manzanita, sprayed black
 Petunia foliage

CONTAINER: Anodized aluminum compote
BASE: Black glass
MECHANICS: Needlepoint holder
SIZE: *Height*: 31 inches, *Width*: 25 inches

MATERIALS:
Moss
Orchid foliage
Orchids—Cymbidiums

CONTAINER: Hollow tree trunk
BASE: Cork
MECHANICS: Aquapics
SIZE: *Height:* 28 inches, *Width:* 26 inches

PLATE 22

Cymbidiums

A spray of delicate pink cymbidiums shown as if they were growing from a tree trunk, waxed and polished, gives them a chance to display their grace and beauty. Their own foliage is the second material. Soft green moss surrounds the base of the container.

PLATE 23

Chrysanthemums

Magnolia leaves, glycerinized, are placed in the center of a deep black ceramic bowl and supported by the reeds of horsetail (Equisetum). The single daisy-type chrysanthemums are added next and then the large mums, five in number, are placed to form an incomplete circle which does not hide the edge of the bowl. This is a pleasing arrangement for a low table where one looks down into the design.

MATERIALS:

Chrysanthemums—white
Horsetails (Equisetum)
Magnolia leaves

CONTAINER: Black bowl
MECHANICS: Needlepoint holder
SIZE: *Height*: 32 inches, *Width*: 16 inches

PLATE 24

Designed for a Coffee Table

A polished tree root, pine branches, and marigolds fresh from the garden make a pleasing horizontal design when placed in an iron Korean *usubata* and shown at below eye level.

This arrangement would withstand hot weather, as marigolds have great lasting quality. Carnations could also be used in the same manner and very beautiful color effects obtained with them.

MATERIALS:
  Marigolds   CONTAINER: Iron Korean *usubata*
  Pine branches   MECHANICS: Needlepoint holder
  Tree root   SIZE: *Height*: 17 inches, *Width*: 28 inches

MATERIALS:
  Velvet rose—Aeonium canariense
  Horsetails (Equisetum)
  Manzanita, sprayed black
  Pine

CONTAINER: Brass and silver vase
BASE: Teakwood
MECHANICS: Vase filled with wet Oasis
SIZE: *Height:* 36 inches, *Width:* 24 inches

PLATE 25

Designed for a Library

One beautifully grown succulent known as a velvet rose—Aeonium canariense—brings drama to a modern design. The branch of manzanita, sprayed black, is shaped almost like the bird design that is shown on the container. A diagonal thrust of horsetails (Equisetum) and two branches of pine give balance to the composition.

MATERIALS:
Gypsophila—pink
Lily—Eucharis

CONTAINER: Clam shell
BASE: Glass
MECHANICS: Needlepoint holder
SIZE: *Height*: 35 inches, *Width*: 45 inches

PLATE 26

Summertime

Designed for a tea table for the bride-to-be.

A bronze figure of a girl with flowers in her hands to represent cymbals seems to be dancing through a mist of pink gypsophila. The great clam shell with its pink pearl lining adds color. The arrangement rests on a thick glass base which returns an enchanting reflection. Cloth—pale pink organdy over taffeta.

PLATE 27

A white china bowl of interesting pattern needs very little material to make a pleasing arrangement. Five white carnations and the stylized foliage of the yucca complement each other. Great simplicity makes this effective.

A design such as this placed where a beam of light falls on it enhances the ethereal quality that a white arrangement seems to project.

MATERIALS:
Carnations   CONTAINER: White china bowl   MECHANICS: Needlepoint holder
Yucca leaves   BASE: White glass   SIZE: *Height:* 22½ inches, *Width:* 9 inches

PLATE 28

Designed for a Modern Setting

Three spikes of gladiolus, a branch of pine, and a very interesting root inserted in a fine old incense burner make a handsome arrangement.

MATERIALS:
    Gladiolus
    Pine branch
    Root

CONTAINER: Bronze incense burner
BASE: Teakwood

ACCESSORY: A colorful old mandarin jacket
MECHANICS: Needlepoint holder
SIZE: *Height*: 30 inches, *Width*: 16 inches

67

MATERIALS:
    Nandina
    Roses—Orange Delight

CONTAINER: Dull gold Chinese lacquered vase
BASE: Teakwood
MECHANICS: Wire mesh
SIZE: *Height*: 50 inches, *Width*: 25 inches

PLATE 29

Designed to Stand on the Floor

Nandina is a beautiful berried shrub, native to China and Japan, which grows well in our warmer climates. The large clusters of berries, when ripe, are a brilliant red. In this arrangement the berries were just beginning to ripen so that the color of the berries ranged from a light yellow to a red-orange. The roses are the Orange Delight. A beautiful combination of material.

MATERIALS:
    Aeonium canariense
    Palm leaf, sprayed black

CONTAINER: Tall cylindrical vase of green pottery
BASE: Black glass
MECHANICS: Vase filled with wet sand
SIZE: *Height*: 20 inches, *Width*: 21 inches

PLATE 30

A handsome succulent, Aeonium canariense, 7 inches in diameter and a palm leaf in its embryo stage of development make an arresting modern design. The palm leaf, which has been sprayed black, resembles a large humming bird. Startling at first and yet interesting and original. The vase is filled with wet sand which keeps the plant fresh and beautiful for many weeks.

70

PLATE 31

First Breath of Spring

A nest made of pussy willow becomes an original container for the first daffodils.

MATERIALS: CONTAINER: Cupped needlepoint holder
  Daffodils   BASE: Wooden pedestal
  Pussy willow   SIZE: *Height:* 28 inches, *Width:* 18 inches

PLATE 32

Planned for a Coffee Table

The second flowering of your favorite delphinium arrives at the same time as the chrysanthemums appear in our markets. Six Fuji mums and six slender spikes of delphinium fit gracefully into a deep glass modern bowl. Several dried palm spikes, bleached white, give a flair to the design. Designed to be seen from all sides.

MATERIALS:
  Chrysanthemums—Fuji
  Delphinium
  Palm spikes

CONTAINER: Swedish glass bowl
BASE: 10-inch square of glass
MECHANICS: Round needlepoint holder
SIZE: *Height:* 18 inches, *Width:* 10 inches

PLATE 33

Contemporary

Potted plants lend themselves to an arrangement when flowers are sometimes difficult to obtain. Here an offshoot of the air plant, billbergia, and a broken stem of a begonia produce an arrangement with an Oriental flair. The container is a piece of modern Oriental pottery. With adequate water in the container and an occasional spray of lukewarm water, a design such as this will last for weeks in the wintertime.

MATERIALS: CONTAINER: Black pottery compote
    Begonia   MECHANICS: Needlepoint holder
    Billbergia   SIZE: *Height:* 18 inches, *Width:* 10 inches

MATERIALS:
　　Cecropia leaves
　　Chrysanthemums—yellow
　　Spathodea pods

CONTAINER: Aluminum extrusion
MECHANICS: Aquapics. Dried material was taped to
　　the extrusion.
SIZE: *Height:* 42 inches, *Width:* 20 inches

PLATE 34

Designed for a Reception Area in an Office Building

An aluminum extrusion was used for the container. Dried material with a fresh accent was chosen for easy maintenance. The flowers are in separate Aquapics and can be easily replaced.

MATERIALS:
  Coral
  Dried grasses
  Driftwood
  Pine

CONTAINER: Driftwood
MECHANICS: Needlepoint holder
SIZE: *Height*: 24 inches, *Width*: 20 inches

PLATE 35

Designed for a Low Glass Table

An interesting piece of wood makes an unusual container for a piece of white coral and one of the lovely grasses.

MATERIALS:
Canna buds
Canna leaves
Gladiolus
Papyrus

CONTAINER: Grecian libation cup
MECHANICS: Needlepoint holder and wire mesh
SIZE: *Height*: 23 inches, *Width*: 11 inches

PLATE 36 *(right)*

For a Man's Office

A reproduction of a Grecian libation cup is a challenging container. It is made of iron and finished in antique gold. Canna leaves are so placed that they act as a shield for the papyrus that is dried but still has retained lovely shades of tan and rose, and for the dark red tips of the canna buds. The full-blown gladiolus flowers bring forth a splash of deep pink. The design is strong, bold, and well balanced. Can be seen from all sides with an entirely different interest on the reverse side.

MATERIALS:
Hydrangea
Sedum
Yucca

CONTAINER: Oriental ceramic vase
MECHANICS: Wet sand
SIZE: *Height*: 28 inches, *Width*: 10 inches

PLATE 37 *(far right)*

A Perpendicular Design

A tall Oriental ceramic vase in unusual tones of gray harmonizes with the plant material shown. One tall spike of yucca in seed, two blossoms of the common hydrangea (*H. paniculata grandiflora*), and a cutting from one of the sedums make an interesting, long-lasting arrangement.

80

MATERIALS:
  Delphiniums—Pacific hybrid
  Roses—Floribunda—Snow Queen

CONTAINER: Alabaster
MECHANICS: Crumpled wire mesh
SIZE: *Height:* 72 inches, *Width:* 48 inches

PLATE 38

There is no blue like the blue cup
The tall delphinium holds up,
Not sky, nor distant hill, nor sea,
Sapphire, nor lapis lazuli.
LOUISE DRISCOLL
from "MY GARDEN IS A PLEASANT PLACE"

A tall arrangement designed to stand on the floor in a modern setting.

MATERIALS:
  Daffodils
  Silverleaf—Leucadendron

CONTAINER: Lamp base
MECHANICS: Needlepoint holder
SIZE: *Height:* 40 inches, *Width:* 27 inches

PLATE 39

In an old lamp base daffodils and silverleaf (Leucadendron) make a charming picture. The heavy perpendicular line formed by the silverleaf is relieved by the beauty of its silk velvety texture. The diagonal line makes one feel as though the daffodils were in motion.

PLATE 40

A columnar arrangement, architectural in feeling. Great depth was achieved by surrounding the column of white gladiolus with canna leaves. Tall and inspirational, it was designed for an altar.

MATERIALS:
   Canna leaves—dark
   Gladiolus—white

CONTAINER: Black chalice
MECHANICS: Needlepoint holder
SIZE: *Height:* 40 inches, *Width:* 15 inches

86

PLATE 41

The same setting as shown in Plate 26, substituting the Chinese figure for the dancing girl. The design could be called "Mist." In this picture the gypsophila is white.

MATERIALS:
  Gypsophila—white
  Lilies—Eucharis

CONTAINER: Clam shell
BASE: Glass
MECHANICS: Needlepoint holder
SIZE: *Height:* 35 inches, *Width:* 45 inches

87

MATERIALS:
Lycoris

CONTAINER: Hollow tree trunk, waxed and polished
MECHANICS: Needlepoint holder
SIZE: *Height:* 26 inches, *Width:* 15 inches

PLATE 42

A hollow tree trunk, waxed and polished, makes a beautiful container for the summer amaryllis (Lycoris). The color of the flower is lilac-pink. The straplike leaves of this lovely flower appear in the spring and then completely die down before the tall spikes of flowers appear in August and September.

PLATE 43

A delicate pattern is created by using three long stems of the angel-wing begonia in perfect blossom. Some leaves were removed to dramatize the floral pendants. A diagonal line formed by a branch of manzanita adds distinction and originality. The flowers were cherry red, the container black glass.

MATERIALS:
   Begonia—angel-wing
   Manzanita

CONTAINER: Black glass vase
MECHANICS: Oasis that has been soaked in water
SIZE: *Height:* 30 inches, *Width:* 30 inches

90

PLATE 44

A pine root sculptured by Nature and a fungous growth black as ink found on a tree in the mountains make a dramatic holder for the two bright red anthurium flowers and foliage. It is so beautifully simple that one has the feeling that this spot was where the flowers grew.

MATERIALS:
  Anthurium
  Anthurium foliage

CONTAINER: Pine root and fungus
MECHANICS: Cupped needlepoint holder
SIZE: *Height*: 36 inches, *Width*: 24 inches

MATERIALS:
Loquat
Scotch broom

CONTAINER: Black marble vase
MECHANICS: Needlepoint holder
SIZE: *Height:* 38 inches, *Width:* 38 inches

PLATE 45

Loquat in Bloom

The beautiful foliage of the loquat that grows so luxuriantly in the South is one of our favorite ornamental shrubs. It is shown here in full bloom with clusters of creamy, fragrant flowers. Scotch broom was used for contrast.

MATERIALS:
   Poppies—May Curtis (flowers, buds, and foliage)

CONTAINER: Black bowl
BASE: Oriental stand
MECHANICS: Needlepoint holder
SIZE: *Height:* 32 inches, *Width:* 16 inches

PLATE 46

Poppies

Simplicity speaks for itself. Three full-blown poppies, American Beauty in color, and three buds make a lovely arrangement. The gray green of poppy foliage is complementary to the exquisite flower. Newly opened flowers cut late in the day and quickly placed in cool, deep water for several hours will be well conditioned and ready for arranging.

PLATE 47

Celosia and Austrian Pine

MATERIALS:
    Celosia—deep rose
    Pine—Austrian

CONTAINER: Modern green pottery
MECHANICS: Oasis
SIZE: *Height:* 23 inches, *Width:* 15 inches

PLATE 48

A Modern Design in an Old Chinese Container

Scotch broom separates the flowers from the foliage of the billbergia plant to give this interesting effect. The color of these pendant flowers is bright blue and green. One of our exotic plant materials.

MATERIALS:
  Billbergia
  Scotch broom

CONTAINER: Chinese vase
MECHANICS: Wet sand
BASE: Teakwood

SIZE: *Height:* 42 inches, *Width:* 24 inches

MATERIALS:
   Pine branch and tips
   Roses

CONTAINER: Oriental metal planter
MECHANICS: Needlepoint holder
SIZE: *Height:* 10 inches, *Width:* 7 inches

PLATE 49

Pine and Roses

A simple design in an Oriental container. Pine is one of our long-lasting plant materials. One branch with several tips of pine impaled on a needlepoint holder remains in perfect condition for a long time. Replace the fresh flowers as often as they are needed.

PLATE 50

Modern

A bleached tree root makes a handsome container for the exotic flower, bird-of-paradise (Strelitzia), with its own handsome foliage.

MATERIALS:
Bird-of-paradise flower
Bird-of-paradise foliage

CONTAINER: Driftwood
ACCESSORIES: Small, smooth black stones
MECHANICS: Concealed cupped needlepoint holder
SIZE: *Height*: 33 inches, *Width*: 25 inches

PLATE 51

An Effective Use of Flowering Plants

A white sculptured figurine stands on a black pedestal within a black niche. Echeveria in full flower makes a lovely frame. Wet sand will keep this reliable plant fresh for several weeks. The flowers are coral in color and contrast well with the steel-gray of the leaves. Echeveria is easily propagated by rooting the leaves in sand.

MATERIALS:
   Echeveria metalica

CONTAINER: Cupped needlepoint holders
ACCESSORIES: Figurine, pedestal, and niche
SIZE: *Height*: 30 inches, *Width*: 12 inches

PLATE 52

Modern Design for a Buffet Table

An original ceramic container in a soft yellow-green glaze with a lining of yellow glaze was designed for fruit. Filled with pears and apples, it became gay and whimsical when a tail of plant material was added.

MATERIALS:

Apples	Fantazma palm	CONTAINER: Ceramic bird
Billbergia	Pears	MECHANICS: None
Date florets	Tradescantia	SIZE: *Height:* 27 inches, *Width:* 21 inches

MATERIALS:
    Heart of yucca
    Limes
    Peaches
    Plums
    Watermelon—miniature

CONTAINER: Black ceramic compote
MECHANICS: Needlepoint holder for yucca
SIZE: *Height:* 34 inches, *Width:* 17 inches

PLATE 53

Sculpture Using Fruit

Shown on a glass-topped table. The sculptured forms of fruit and melons lend themselves to a modern design so popular today. A design showing restraint and lovely color harmony.

MATERIALS:
　　Coconut in husks
　　Coconut spathes
　　Horsetails (Equisetum)
　　Scouring rush (Equisetum hyemale)

CONTAINER: Cupped needlepoint holder
BASE: Bamboo mat
SIZE: *Height:* 26 inches, *Width:* 20 inches

PLATE 54

For the patio, designed to withstand the outdoor summer weather.

MATERIALS:
  Gladiolus—red
  Savoy cabbage leaves

CONTAINER: Metal planter
MECHANICS: Needlepoint holder
SIZE: *Height:* 19 inches, *Width:* 10 inches

PLATE 55

Savoy cabbage leaves, beautiful in color and texture, when combined with bright red gladiolus make a delightful summer table arrangement.

To condition the cabbage, soak the leaves in 2 gallons of water to which a cup of cider vinegar has been added. Let stand overnight. The leaves will be crisp and easy to arrange.

MATERIALS:
    Bananas—green
    Grapes—Ribier
    Roses—yellow

CONTAINER: Natural wood
MECHANICS: Oasis
SIZE: *Height:* 10 inches, *Length:* 18 inches

PLATE 56

Fruit and Roses in One of Nature's Containers

The texture and color of this lovely piece of wood looked like engraved silver.

PLATE 57

Purple cabbage leaves and lavender chrysanthemums make an attractive table arrangement. Cabbage leaves must be conditioned. Soaked for several hours in 2 gallons of water to which 1 cup of vinegar has been added, the leaves become so crisp that they remain lovely for several days.

MATERIALS:
   Cabbage leaves—purple
   Chrysanthemums—lavender

CONTAINER: Purple plate
MECHANICS: Cupped needlepoint holder
SIZE: *Height*: 19 inches, *Width*: 12 inches

PLATE 58

Three gourds and small bright red peppers make this an arrangement of line, form, and distinction. In fact, placed on a base of white marble it appears quite elegant. Seeing Nature's wonderful sculpture in these simple vegetables is true awareness.

MATERIALS:
  Gourds
  Peppers

CONTAINER: None
BASE: White marble
SIZE: *Height*: 25 inches, *Width*: 20 inches

MATERIALS:
  Gourd (about 10 inches high and about 8 inches wide)
  Goldenrod
  Osmanthus
  Scotch broom
  Thistle

CONTAINER: Cupped needlepoint holder
BASE: Bamboo mat
SIZE: *Height:* 37 inches, *Width:* 20 inches

PLATE 59

This gourd so resembled a swan that to me it was fantastic. For a table arrangement in the fall nothing could be more suitable. Scotch broom that has been chemically treated is new on the market. It is quite beautiful, with a rich brown color, and is pliable and easy to use. A soft loop of the broom seems to emphasize the shape of the "swan's" neck. Goldenrod and a branch of osmanthus give depth to the design, but the *pièce de résistance* is the yellow thistle. Humorous, yet pleasing. Try it!

MATERIALS:
    Haole seed pods
    Pattypan squash
    Wheat

CONTAINER: Dried gourd
MECHANICS: None
SIZE: *Height:* 16 inches, *Width:* 30 inches

PLATE 60

A dried gourd sawed in half and painted black makes an original container for vegetables. Here three pattypan squash fill the bowl. Golden wheat with a ribbon bow of haole seed pods from Hawaii forms the diagonal line. Delightfully effective in a sophisticated manner.

MATERIALS:
    Bamboo reeds
    Helianthus—Autumnal
    Sunflowers in seed

MECHANICS: Cupped needlepoint holder
SIZE: *Height*: 40 inches, *Width*: 30 inches

PLATE 61

A table design for the bird watcher's brunch. Sunflowers, with seeds almost ripe, are set on edge to represent a container. The radiating line is formed by bamboo reeds. The flower is another member of the sunflower family, Helianthus Autumnal. The table covering is a bamboo mat.

PLATE 62

Designed for a Golden Anniversary Table

Two Venetian glass birds with touches of gold face each other with their beaks partly hidden by the overflow of flowers and fruit. The table covering is of white nylon over yellow silk.

MATERIALS:
Apricots
Begonia leaves
Bouvardia

Broom, sprayed gold
Grapes
Roses—miniature, yellow

CONTAINER: Glass birds
BASE: Glass
MECHANICS: Wire mesh
SIZE: *Height:* 30 inches, *Width:* 30 inches

MATERIALS:
Alligator pear
Cattails—miniature
Diablo pods
Fruit of the flowering quince
Horsechestnuts
Ipomoea (Hawaiian
    morning-glory) seeds
Palm spikes
Zucchini

PLATE 63

Arrangement for an Office in the Alcoa Building, Pittsburgh

An autumn arrangement showing the expressive power of line. Here the vertical, diagonal, and curved lines are all combined to produce this composition of interesting materials. The rare black glass container shaped like a bird presented a challenge. The reflection in the clear glass squares over black Carrara glass added interest.

CONTAINER: Black glass bird
BASE: Black Carrara rectangle and clear glass squares

MECHANICS: Dry sand
SIZE: *Height*: 26 inches, *Width*: 24 inches

PLATE 64 *(above)*

The Awareness of Texture

One luscious melon whose surface structure is such a perfect example to illustrate *rough* texture. The dried spathodea pods sprayed black and the black coconut spathe used for a container make an original centerpiece for the summertime. The melon makes the ideal dessert after a barbecue party.

MATERIALS:
Melon
Spathodea pods

CONTAINER: Coconut spathe
MECHANICS: None
SIZE: *Height:* 16 inches, *Width:* 30 inches

PLATE 65 *(opposite page)*

For the luncheon table. A delightful idea that can be executed the day before a party. A brandy snifter is filled with marigolds and limes. A piece of Oasis two inches square and as long as the depth of the bowl is cut from a *soaked* block of Oasis. Using the Oasis as the center of your design, first press the flower heads into the Oasis in rows, then place the limes in rows. Five rows of flowers and four of limes perfectly filled a snifter 10 inches high with a bowl that measured 7½ inches deep and 5½ inches wide at the top. Many combinations of flowers and fruits can be used. Pink carnations with plums are lovely, or use red carnations and limes for Christmas. Any long, thin leaves or fern fronds can be used for a top.

SIZE: *Height from back:* 8 inches
Height from front: 6 inches
Width: 12 inches

PLATE 67

Sculpture Using Fruit and Vegetables

The unusual iron container was created from salvaged material. The bowl was originally the catch basin of an umbrella stand which was in fashion probably in the late 'nineties. The base was formed from two feet belonging to an old iron bathtub. The feet were turned upside down and welded to the bottom of the basin, thus producing one of my favorite containers. Especially nice for fruit and vegetables.

MATERIALS: CONTAINER: Iron compote
  Apples   Grapes MECHANICS: One Aquapic for green leaves
  Billbergia Peppers SIZE: *Height:* 21 inches, *Width:* 18 inches

PLATE 68

"When the Frost Is on the Pumpkin"

A wooden bowl, large enough to hold a 10-inch pumpkin, was chosen as the container for a Thanksgiving Eve supper party. Cornstalks with beautiful tassels were cut from a late variety of corn. They were kept fresh and green by putting them in a large plastic bag and storing in a cool root cellar. Hickory nuts still in their outer shell were clustered to give balance to the pumpkin. Special spot lighting threw fantastic shadows on the wall. The cloth was homespun linen tinted a very light tan.

MATERIALS:
  Cornstalks
  Hickory nuts
  Pumpkin

CONTAINER: Wooden bowl
MECHANICS: Needlepoint holder
SIZE: *Height:* 23 inches, *Width:* 13 inches

PLATE 69

Rhythm

Shallot, an onionlike plant that grows in this fantastic pattern, was chosen to portray rhythmic motion. Rhythm, one of the principles of design, is so often produced in an obvious manner that the true effect of motion is lost. Seek, then, material that expresses rhythm or motion in natural growth that needs no contrivance or distortion. Perhaps more than any other factor rhythm can lend distinction to an arrangement, so strive to achieve it; it is worth the effort.

The container is a fungous growth from a South American tree. One could mistake it for a wood-carving. The arrangement rests on a rectangle of black glass.

MATERIALS: CONTAINER: Fungus   MECHANICS: Needlepoint holder
  Shallots   BASE: Black glass   SIZE: *Height*: 34 inches, *Width*: 24 inches

MATERIALS:
  Chestnuts
  Crab apples
  Grapes
  Moss juniper
  Pine cones
  Plums
  Raffia
  Seckel pears
  Strawberry corn
  Wheat

CONTAINER: Antique chalice
MECHANICS: Dowel stick, wire, and floral clay
SIZE: *Height*: 30 inches, *Width*: 16 inches

PLATE 70

Thanksgiving

A wire espaliered tree rich in the symbolism and tradition of the holiday. Wheat—the staff of life. Fruits and nuts—the rich harvest of our land. The chalice—religious significance of the day.

The garland of braided raffia—a family united by many strands of affection.

The cloth of homespun with the motto "Give Us This Day Our Daily Bread" was designed by Betty Abel.

MATERIALS:
Plum branches
Roses—hybrid tea
Roses—miniature

CONTAINER: Glass bowl
BASE: Silver
MECHANICS: Needlepoint holder
ACCESSORY: Picture
SIZE: *Height:* 26 inches, *Width:* 26 inches

PLATE 71

Heritage

A special arrangement designed for "Grandmother's day." Here an accessory becomes the most important part of a composition. Deep red hybrid tea roses and miniature red roses make a charming combination for a special day. Curved branches seem to embrace the flowers. The container is an antique cranberry hobnail glass bowl which belonged to the great-grandmother of the child in the picture. The silver frame belonged to the child's great-grandfather, but the child is a first grandchild and he belongs to me.

MATERIALS:
Asparagus Sprengeri
Forget-me-nots
Lilies of the valley
Pansies
Primroses
Roses—miniature
Violets

CONTAINER: Victorian silver compote
ACCESSORY: Fan
MECHANICS: Needlepoint holder
SIZE: *Height*: 22 inches, *Width*: 27 inches

PLATE 72

A Victorian Reminiscence

Designed for a tea table. A Victorian fan of Duchesse lace is an accessory used as an integral part of the composition. The cloth is of blue satin.

MATERIALS:
Lily—auratum
Pine tips

CONTAINER: Green glass bottle
BASE: Root and pine
MECHANICS: None
SIZE: *Height*: 36 inches, *Width*: 21 inches

PLATE 73

A bridal table designed for a garden party. Only one stem of the spectacular auratum lily was placed in a chartreuse-green bottle to show off its aristocratic beauty. The bottle was then given an outdoor type of setting using a tree root and tips of the long-needle pine for a base which blended perfectly into its surroundings. The tablecloth was chartreuse green.

MATERIALS:
Asparagus—Sprengeri
Roses—miniature
Tuberoses

CONTAINER: Crystal candelabrum
MECHANICS: Oasis
SIZE: *Height*: 36 inches, *Width*: 18 inches

PLATE 74

Tea Table Design

A crystal candelabrum was used for a container. Stems of tuberoses were used instead of candles to create this charming and feminine arrangement. Miniature roses and the asparagus fern Sprengeri increased the beauty of this special-occasion design. Oasis soaked in water was cut into rounds to fit the candleholders to keep the flowers fresh and lovely.

137

MATERIALS:
  Almonds
  Coconut calyx
  Eucalyptus pods
  Gardenias
  Honey locust pods
  Peach stones

ACCESSORIES: Bird and plaster model
MECHANICS: Wire frame and wire circle
BASE: Black wood
SIZE: *Height:* 22 inches, *Width:* 22 inches

PLATE 75

A Design for a Mantel at Christmas

The plaster model of the sculpture in Plate 85 made an effective center for a wreath of lovely material. The wreath was sprayed gold and mounted on a black base. Three gardenias added their elegance to a very beautiful Christmas idea.

PLATE 76

Designed for an Altar

MATERIALS:
    Astilbe—white
    Astilbe foliage
    Lily—Madonna or Annunciation

CONTAINER: Stone vase sculptured by Mary Lee Kennedy White
MECHANICS: None (The opening was small enough to hold the stems so securely that mechanics were unnecessary.)
ACCESSORY: Antique Chinese temple screen
SIZE: *Height:* 42 inches, *Width:* 15 inches

MATERIALS:
   Eucalyptus
   Grass
   Holly
   Peppers
   Pheasant feather
   Squash

CONTAINER: Coconut spathe
BASE: Wood
MECHANICS: Needlepoint holder
SIZE: *Height:* 34 inches, *Width:* 26 inches

PLATE 77

Designed for a Bon Voyage Luncheon

In a coconut spathe painted black and mounted on a square wooden base, two unusual squash, deep orange in color, chartreuse green sweet peppers, holly, eucalyptus, and roadside black grass are combined to illustrate a form and texture pattern. For a bit of dash and color, a South American pheasant feather was added.

MATERIALS:
  Artichokes
  Peppers
  Wheat

CONTAINER: Gray ceramic compote
MECHANICS: Dowel stick, clay, and toothpicks
SIZE: *Height*: 35 inches, *Width*: 8 inches

PLATE 78

Come for Cocktails

A tall, slender arrangement that requires very little table space. A dowel stick was thrust through the artichokes which were then spaced evenly along the dowel. Small red peppers were impaled on toothpicks and thrust into the stems of the artichokes in even rows, then the dowel stick was securely fastened into the container. Golden wheat bursts forth at the top and adds a gay touch.

MATERIALS:
Scallions

CONTAINER: Black candlestick
MECHANICS: Ribbon
SIZE: *Height:* 32 inches, *Width:* 8 inches

PLATE 79

Designed for a Barbecue Party

Scallions scrubbed and tied in a bundle with white satin ribbon and mounted in a tall, black candlestick become a striking centerpiece and edible if you please. The denim cloth is half solid green, half green and white stripes. The container at the left was filled with limes and sprigs of mint.

PLATE 80

An amusing arrangement designed for a bachelor's dinner party. The topknots are dried teasels. Red satin ribbon was used for the hair ribbon and fashioned the gentlemen's neckties. Pine tips swirling around the base helped to make the centerpiece gay and festive.

MATERIALS:
Gourds—bright green
Pine tips
Ribbon
Teasels, dried

CONTAINER: None
BASE: Cork
MECHANICS: Pins
SIZE: *Height:* 15 inches, *Width:* 18 inches

PLATE 81

Whimsical

For a buffet table on the patio and the last outdoor party of the season. The pine-cone owl is available commercially, though it would not be difficult to make yourself.

MATERIALS:
  Corn tassels
  Pine-cone owl, 10 inches high
  Strawberry corn

CONTAINER: None
MECHANICS: Needlepoint holder to support owl and
  corn tassels
BASE: Straw mat
SIZE: *Height:* 22 inches, *Width:* 12 inches

MATERIALS:
Parsley
Tomatoes

CONTAINER: Glass bowl
MECHANICS: Styrofoam and toothpicks
BASE: Inverted glass bowl
SIZE: *Height*: 24 inches, *Width*: 10 inches

PLATE 82

An Edible Centerpiece

Small "love apples" (cherry tomatoes) and parsley make a design for a cocktail party that is edible and fun! The tomatoes were impaled on toothpicks which were thrust into a Styrofoam ball. The Styrofoam ball was supported by a dowel stick that had been anchored in a heavy glass bowl. The base is an inverted bowl of the same design only smaller in size. The topknot is of Swedish design.

MATERIALS:
    Aspidistra leaves
    Black beans
    Grains of chicken corn
    Sunflower seeds

CONTAINER: Antique mortar
MECHANICS: Dowel stick, Styrofoam, and clay
SIZE: *Height*: 27 inches, *Width*: 32 inches

PLATE 83

A table arrangement designed for a corn roast. Grains of corn were glued onto a ball of Styrofoam, using a tile mastic. Then a turkey made of black beans, corn, and sunflower seeds was glued on top of the grains of corn, which seemed to make the turkey stand out in relief. When finished, the entire ball was sprayed with clear plastic until it looked as though it were a ball of mosaic tile. A dowel stick, painted black, was used as a stem and securely fastened into the antique mortar. Actually a clay flower pot would be just as attractive. Several of these on a long table, each with a different motif, certainly can add interest to a party. The leaves are from the house plant aspidistra.

MATERIALS:
  Kale
  Onions
  Turnips

CONTAINER: Old lamp base
MECHANICS: Styrofoam, toothpicks, and Aquapic
SIZE: *Height:* 32 inches, *Width:* 15 inches

PLATE 84

Elegance with Vegetables

Red-skinned onions that have sent forth the most fantastic sprouts of chartreuse green, purple and white turnips with their green tops evenly cut, two handsome leaves of kale for a topknot, make a truly spectacular arrangement for a buffet table. A cone of Styrofoam was used as a foundation for the vegetables. The onions and turnips were impaled on toothpicks and stuck into the cone. Kale was kept fresh in an Aquapic filled with water and easily concealed among the vegetables. The base is an old oil lamp made of iron, painted black and sprayed with lacquer.

Here the influence of the Byzantine period can be detected. Seeing the beauty, form, and color in all things is enriching.

MATERIALS:
    Amaryllis leaves
    Iris—Dutch, white
    Pine—Mugho

CONTAINER: Cupped needlepoint holder
BASE: Marble
ACCESSORY: Mahogany carving by Mary Lee
    Kennedy White
SIZE: *Height*: 33 inches, *Width*: 24 inches

PLATE 85

Sculpture and Flowers

A composition inspired by the lovely sculpture of Mother and Child carved in mahogany by Mary Lee Kennedy White. The pure white of the Dutch iris, the opposing lines of amaryllis leaves, and the soft green pine at the base create a thought-provoking picture full of meaning.

MATERIALS:
   Horsetails (Equisetum)
   Lilies—Mid-century

CONTAINER: Bark mounted on a wooden base
MECHANICS: Cupped needlepoint holder
SIZE: *Height*: 30 inches, *Width*: 16 inches

PLATE 86

Madonna of the Garden

Wood, sculptured by the wind and storms, has come to mean much to those of us who are developing awareness of Nature. Each person seems to have a different concept of its beauty. For example, the author sees in this piece of wood a woman's figure kneeling as though in prayer and the piece has for her, therefore, a spiritual value of great beauty.

MATERIALS:
   Bouvardia
   Willow—curly (Salix babylonica crispa)

CONTAINER: Wood
BASE: Cork
MECHANICS: Needlepoint holder
SIZE: *Height*: 36 inches, *Width*: 44 inches

PLATE 87

Awareness

The handsome piece of wood found in the mountains by the author inspired this expressive composition. A great bird seems to be resting beside a nest that has been so beautifully sculptured by Nature. A figurine of Saint Francis of Assisi, the patron saint of the birds, stands beneath a branch of the curly willow (Salix babylonica crispa), while at his feet small white flowers seem to have burst into bloom. This composition could well be titled "Nesting Time and Spring Have Returned."

MATERIALS:
Lilies—Mid-century

CONTAINER: Feather Rock
ACCESSORY: Root
SIZE: *Height*: 34 inches, *Width*: 29 inches

PLATE 88

For the Patio

A lava substance known commercially as Feather Rock was chosen to hold a favorite root that was found on a bank of a mountain stream. The lilies (Mid-century) were solidly grouped to form a strong perpendicular line in direct contrast to the flowing, graceful curve of the root. Notice how the root enfolded the large, smooth pebble which was in its pathway of growth. How privileged is one to see and be aware of these treasures and miracles of Nature. Forceful, dynamic and suitable for an outdoor arrangement. The soft spring green in the background comes and goes so quickly that it seems like magic. Shown on a glass-topped table with a base of Nature's sculptured wood.

DESIGNS FOR EXHIBITIONS

PLATE 89

Designed for a class in a flower show which called for a composition featuring an unusual piece of driftwood. Both fresh and dry materials were permitted. Staged on two levels of cork, this very modern arrangement could be used in a reception room in one of our modern office buildings.

MATERIALS:
  Boxwood
  Broom corn, dried
  Driftwood
  Chrysanthemums—white

CONTAINER: None
BASE: Cork
MECHANICS: Aquapics and needlepoint holder
SIZE: *Height:* 36 inches, *Width:* 36 inches

MATERIALS:
  Cattails—tan
  Chestnuts in outer covering
  Chrysanthemums
  Coconuts in their husks
  Coconut spathes
  Cotton in pods
  Fern fronds
  Horsetails (Equisetum)
  Mullein

CONTAINER: Alabaster
MECHANICS: Wire mesh and orchid tubes
BASE: Marble
SIZE: *Height:* 72 inches, *Width:* 30 inches

PLATE 90

Designed for the Board Room of the Alcoa Building, Pittsburgh

Since the design was to last for many weeks and because the space to be filled required an arrangement 72 inches tall, dried materials were chosen and a design constructed so that a fresh material accent could be added whenever necessary.

The colors in the modern painting to the left of the arrangement were tan, brown, black, and white. The wood paneling back of the design was of rosewood. The materials chosen were of the same color harmony, with the green of the horsetails on the left the only contrasting color. The light tan of the tall cattails was particularly beautiful. The white mums were kept fresh by using large orchid tubes filled with water, which also made possible the changing of the fresh material without disturbing the arrangement. This was a challenging exhibit.

166

MATERIALS:
  Orchids—Cymbidiums

CONTAINER: None
ACCESSORY: Glass cullet
BASE: Wood
MECHANICS: Aquapic
SIZE: *Height:* 21 inches, *Width:* 15 inches

PLATE 91

For an Exhibition

A large glass cullet was lighted from many angles to produce this magnificent "gem." Spectacular and beautiful when combined with a spray of golden cymbidium orchids. Shown in an exhibit stressing the excitement of glass.

168

MATERIALS:
  Apples
  Chestnuts in burs
  Grapes
  Grasses
  Horsetails (Equisetum)
  Indian corn
  Nectarines
  Peaches
  Pears
  Peppers
  Pine cones
  Plums
  Pomegranates
  Sorghum
  Spiderwort (Tradescantia)
  Wheat

CONTAINER: Green glass bottle
BASE: Round wooden base, painted brown
MECHANICS: Aquapics for the fresh plant material
SIZE: *Height:* 72 inches, *Width:* 24 inches

PLATE 92

End of Summer

Nature's bounty richly nurtured by God's gifts of sun and rain.
MARIA BRISCOE CROKER
from "ON CATOCTIN"

A large green, hand-blown bottle was used to represent the good earth. Within, carefully arranged, are fruits, pine cones, Indian corn, and chestnuts in burs. Coming forth from the top of the container and overflowing are seed pods, grasses, roses, ripened grains, and great bunches of grapes. All this depicts Nature's bounty that has been so richly nurtured, so lavishly given unto us. This is a thought-provoking, beautiful composition of exquisite coloring.

171

PLATE 93

An Exhibition

A magnificently sculptured piece of wood from the Rocky Mountains was displayed in the lobby of the Alcoa Building in Pittsburgh when the building was officially opened. Pale pink and white anthuriums, with their own foliage, together with great bunches of pink and black alabaster grapes formed a picture of Nature's accomplishments to contrast with the setting in a building symbolizing the feats of man's ability.

MATERIALS:
  Grapes—alabaster
  Anthurium foliage
  Anthuriums
  Wood

CONTAINER: Wood
MECHANICS: Aquapics concealed in the wood
BASE: None (The design was displayed on the top
  of the reception desk in the main lobby.)
SIZE: *Height*: 60 inches, *Width*: 56 inches, *Weight*: 300 pounds

172

Part Three

TOMORROW

To him who in the love of Nature holds
Communion with her visible forms, she speaks
A various language; for his gayer hours
She has a voice of gladness, and a smile
And eloquence of beauty, and she glides
Into his darker musings, with a mild
And healing sympathy, that steals away
Their sharpness, ere he is aware. . . .

WILLIAM CULLEN BRYANT
from "THANATOPSIS"

TOMORROW

Three decades is but a short period for the study of any subject. Yet so great has been the interest, the enthusiasm, the growing awareness of beauty in flower design that finally flowers have taken their rightful place in the American field of art.

History has proven that civilization and the awareness of beauty go hand in hand. Today, we are convinced that flowers are no longer a luxury but a necessity for our way of life.

We have studied the floral art of the past. We have developed a new awareness of the beauty around us. We have found that flowers not only have visual loveliness but that they can express *us*—our moods, our emotions, our creativity.

And what is even more wonderful, we all have access to flowers or plant material. This gives to each of us the opportunity to create and to satisfy our need for self-expression. No other art can give so much to so many. The tools with which we work are abundant and many of them free for the picking—tools of color unparalleled in beauty, tools unequaled in sculpture. These are designed for us by the greatest of all Designers.

Could we ask for more?

Let us, then, accept these gifts from God with reverence and respect and use them to create beauty, simplicity, harmony, and expression. Let us have as our goal in the art of flower arranging to give to the world of tomorrow more beauty through flowers. As a reward, you will discover another vital aspect of nature and art, the spiritual element that brings comfort and peace.

MATERIALS:
  Angel hair
  Figurines
  Pussy willow
  Sea lavender

CONTAINER: Plastic balls
SIZE: *Length:* 58 inches, *Width:* 45 inches

PLATE 94

An Interpretation of the Christmas Carol "Joy to the World"

A mobile comprised of clear plastic balls of varying sizes. One of the smallest balls contains a miniature china lamb in a bed of angel hair, the other a blue bird surrounded by angel hair. The next larger three balls contain a dove and two angels. In these, angel hair has been used to give a cloudlike effect. The large plastic ball at the bottom cradles the Christ Child, with dried sea lavender (Limonium) and angel hair, making an enchanting setting. The sea lavender continues up through the design. The rod at the top is fashioned of pussy willow stems. The nylon fishing line that was used to suspend all of the plastic balls was so nearly invisible that the balls seemed to be floating in space. A creative expression, a design that gives forth a message.

MATERIALS:
   Twiggy bush branches covered with witches'-broom
   Dried oak leaves

MECHANICS: Suspended from the ceiling on a nylon
   fishing line
SIZE: *Height:* 25 inches, *Width:* 42 inches

PLATE 95

Awareness and Imagination

This mobile was designed after seeing the beauty of a wild bush growing along the roadside . . . seeing on its branches the little nestlike tufts caused by a curious growth called witches'-broom . . . seeing it, with true awareness, just after it had caught the first flakes of an early snow flurry. With great imagination the forms of deer were cut from two dried oak leaves and appear to be scurrying through the bush for shelter. Designed by Beverly Murdoch for the 1961 Christmas Show of the Pittsburgh Guild of Flower Arrangers.

MATERIALS:
    Pine branches

CONTAINER: A stone sculptured by Nature
ACCESSORIES: Discarded bird's nest
    Wooden bird sculptured by man
BASE: Slate
MECHANICS: Cupped needlepoint holder and floral
    clay
SIZE: *Height:* 15 inches, *Width:* 24 inches

PLATE 96

"Now That Winter Is Gone, Let Us Welcome May."

PLATE 97

Spring

Forget-me-nots there linger,
To full perfection brought.
ALICE E. ALLEN
*from "*MY MOTHER'S GARDEN*"*

MATERIALS:
   Horsetails (Equisetum)
   Iris—Dutch
   Iris foliage

CONTAINER: Wood
MECHANICS: Cupped needlepoint holder
SIZE: *Height:* 33 inches, *Width:* 22 inches

A sculptured figure of a Madonna stands in a garden surrounded by forget-me-nots.

183

PLATE 98

"Green Grows the Holly"

A sculptured figure in a meditative mood stands in front of a slab of bark. The branch of holly is heavy with scarlet berries contrasting with the shiny dark green holly leaves. At the base, twigs of spiraea Vanhouttei were used to make a man-made nest. A bark base supports the entire composition. Polished pebbles of many shades of gray add contrast of color and texture.

MATERIALS:
Holly

CONTAINER: Cupped needlepoint holder
BASE: Bark
ACCESSORIES: Figurine, pebbles, and twig nest
SIZE: *Height*: 28 inches, *Width*: 18 inches

PLATE 99

"Our Troubled Country—Christmas, 1963

A cullet of optical glass was used to represent our country—shiny, bright, young, and beautiful. Manzanita branches were sprayed black to represent the troubled areas and dangers that seem to surround us. White gladiolus in the line of inspiration, the perpendicular line, were selected to represent our faith in God. The glass figurine of a woman represents the spirit of America. And because it was Christmas, a branch of holly was added. This is the type of composition we are striving to create—a design that will speak for us when words come not too readily to our lips. This could be one of our designs for tomorrow, a real challenge for self-expression.

MATERIALS:
   Gladiolus—white
   Holly
   Manzanita, sprayed black

CONTAINER: Cupped needlepoint holder
BASE: Cork
ACCESSORIES: Glass Madonna and cullet
SIZE: *Height:* 28 inches, *Width:* 18 inches

185

PLATE 100

187

Easter Morning

GLOSSARY

ACCENT. A special emphasis on a particular flower or flowers, color or form.

ACCESSORY. Anything used in creating an exhibit in addition to the plant material, the container, and the base or fabric on which the container may stand.

ANGEL HAIR. Spun fiber glass.

APPURTENANCES. Accessories or properties used as adjuncts to the major objects in an arrangement.

AQUAPIC. A small plastic device designed to hold water and to hold stems in place.

AWARENESS. Possessing knowledge, being conscious of, *seeing*.

BALANCE. A matter of weight, actual and visual.

BEAUTY. The appeal of the arrangement to the observer.

COLOR. The most compelling element in flower arrangement. A property or quality of visible phenomena distinct from form and from light.

COMPOSITION. A floral arrangement with or without accessories.

CONTAINER. Any receptacle for plant material.

CONTRAST. Unification of opposing elements. A dominant feature is emphasized by means of the difference between it and other elements used near it.

CULLET. Broken or refuse glass which is left over in the course of the manufacture of glass objects.

CUPPED NEEDLEPOINT HOLDER. A holder that serves as a container.

DESIGN. Design in a flower arrangement must include three factors: *space* occupied by the arrangement; the *composition* within that space; the *lines* within that composition.

DIAGONAL LINE. A straight line passing from one angle to any other angle not adjacent.

DOWEL STICK. A round wooden rod.

DRIFTWOOD. Wood worn by water and the elements of weather.

EPERGNE. A centerpiece for table decoration consisting of several receptacles of different sizes grouped together in an ornamental design.

EXPRESSION. The creative quality in a flower arrangement which conveys to the observer an idea, feeling, mood, or story. The quality that makes an arrangement true art.

FLORAL CLAY. A commercial plastic clay used to stabilize needlepoint holders.

FORM. The shape resulting from the structural lines of an arrangement.

HAOLE. A Hawaiian seed pod.

HARMONY. The interrelationship of the component parts in a unified whole.

HORIZONTAL LINE. A line parallel to the base.

LIBATION CUP. A cup used in Ancient Greece for pouring liquid such as wine onto the ground in honor of a deity.

LIKNON. A winnowing fan in the form of a wide basket used in Ancient Greece to hold fruit and flowers.

LIVING LINE. True to life.

MOBILE. A composition designed to have freedom of motion.

MONOCHROMATIC. Consisting of one color.

NEEDLEPOINT HOLDER. A device to hold material in place.

OASIS. A plastic material whose purpose is to hold material in position and, when water-soaked, to keep cut plant material fresh.

ORCHID TUBES. Small glass tubes that hold the stems of flowers in water.

PATTERN. The outline or silhouette, consisting of voids and solids.

PERPENDICULAR LINE. An upright or vertical line. In flower arrangements known as the inspirational line.

PLANT MATERIAL. Anything that grows. Can be fresh or dried.

PROPORTION. The relationship of one part of an arrangement to another. For instance, the height of the arrangement is governed by either the height or the width of the container; whichever of the container's measurements is the greater will become the governing one. The *approximate* ratio is 1½ (the arrangement) to 1 (the container), depending on the material chosen.

RADIATING LINES. Direct lines issuing from a point in the design.

RHYTHM. A feeling of motion in an arrangement which carries the eye through the design. Rhythm can be created by the use of repetition and transition.

RIKKWA STYLE. The first formal style of Japanese floral art.

SCALE. The size-relationship of the component parts.

SIMPLICITY. The elimination of all unnecessary detail.

SILHOUETTE. The pattern of the outline of an arrangement.

SPATHE. Large sheathing bracts of certain plants. That of the coconut palm is often used in flower arrangements.

STYROFOAM. A plastic material used as an aid in flower arranging. Especially useful for dried material.

SYMBOLISM. The use of something to stand meaningfully for something else.

TEXTURE. The tissue structure of plant material.

TRANSITION. A gradual change in size, color, or form.

USUBATA. An early Oriental bronze container with a circular top.

VOIDS. Spaces between the solids in a flower arrangement.

WIRE MESH. Any pliable wire of 1-inch (or more) mesh that can be easily crumpled.

PHOTOGRAPHER'S NOTE

The color photographs in this book were made with 8- x 10-inch transparency films. The lighting was done mainly with incandescent spotlights. The backgrounds, in a few cases, were helped with color gelatins. A 12-inch Ektar and a 20-inch Artar lens were used.

My usual procedure in photographing the arrangements was to help Mrs. Lowry by providing her with a work area and then to stay out of her way. She would arrive at the studio laden with flowers, vases, her tools, and would quickly start working. She worked rapidly and with a minimum of indecision. When she was finished, we placed the arrangement on a plain background and examined it. We would discuss it and agree on what accessories and backgrounds would best complement the flowers.

I would then make the photographic setup and light the flowers as I thought best. Then I would shoot a test transparency and process it. In about an hour, Mrs. Lowry and I could examine the test and make corrections in the setup where necessary. Then I would expose the finished set of transparencies.

The photographic thinking was basic—"keep things simple and above all allow the flowers to dominate."

HAROLD CORSINI

This book was designed by Stefan Salter, and set in Fairfield,
a type face by Rudolph Ruzicka, noted American artist. The
paper is Mead Richgloss Offset Enamel, the printing was done
by Fairfield Lithograph Corporation in Stamford, Connecticut,
and the binding by The Cornwall Press, Inc.